THE BASELINE OF LEADERSHIP

THE BASELINE OF LEADERSHIP

Practical Concepts for Effective Performance and Life Success

by

Anthony L. Johnson, PhD

&

Cynthia F. Johnson, MPA

XULON PRESS

Xulon Press
2301 Lucien Way #415
Maitland, FL 32751
407.339.4217
www.xulonpress.com

© 2018 by Anthony L. Johnson, PhD & Cynthia F. Johnson, MPA

All rights reserved solely by the author. The author guarantees all contents are original and do not infringe upon the legal rights of any other person or work. No part of this book may be reproduced in any form without the permission of the author. The views expressed in this book are not necessarily those of the publisher.

Unless otherwise indicated, Scripture quotations taken from the Holy Bible, New International Version (NIV). Copyright © 1973, 1978, 1984, 2011 by Biblica, Inc.™. Used by permission. All rights reserved.

Printed in the United States of America.

ISBN-13: 978-1-54562-820-1

LEADERSHIP MANTRA

Leadership Development is like the conception, growth, and birth of a child; its being forms within a time capsule of sacrifice, concern, expectancy and expression; its birth begins with a connection between an idea and a desire; and its purpose is evidenced through an open channel of understanding, execution and continual communication within a world for all humankind.

— Anthony L. Johnson, PhD

ACKNOWLEDGEMENTS

We wish to acknowledge you, the leader as you apply the insight from this book in your daily life settings. We acknowledge you for your commitment and dedication to personal growth, team collaboration, organizational development, success, and life fulfillment.

ABOUT THE BOOK

Leadership is a philosophy, evaluating the past and initiating purpose in the present to evolve a unique and progressive phenomenon as the future. Unbeknownst to many, leadership is a gift bestowed upon all in the form of our opportunity to evolve daily. However, it appears the concept of leadership lies dormant as decisions are often contemplated and made void of in-depth critical analysis. The actions in many ways have left progress fragmented and individuals distant from goal achievement. Perhaps we have some commonality in that we ponder questions regarding the potential of leadership. Leadership is more than a thought or idea but a responsibility to personal development and intellectual expansion. Moreover, leadership is a collaboration of commitment to strategy, structure, and service to others. When you think about leadership, what is missing in your life? What aspects can be addressed or acquired to generate or expand your success personally and professionally?

The Baseline of Leadership is essential for emergent leadership as it will foster quality, commitment, efficacy and creativity within your life to evoke performance improvement and goal achievement. *The Baseline of Leadership* is for all who desire to invest their skills into a leadership framework which embodies critical analysis and concrete steps for vision manifestation. As each day, week, and month unfolds in your life, you will receive seeds of influence to expand your capacity to see possibilities, embrace challenges, and release untapped potential for ongoing success. The concepts are not all inclusive as many more themes exist which relate to the holdings of effective and influential leadership. In respect, the selected terms will initiate and increase your perspective of sound decision making and transform you into a model of effective leadership in each venue of your life. In all, we encourage you to take this journey as a path of personal and professional development to connect you to success and victory in life which evidences leadership which is real but uncommon.

HOW TO USE THE BOOK

The Baseline of Leadership is designed as an interactive study of goals, internal analysis, decision-making and achievement. Each chapter presents a door for the reader to enter referencing core themes reflective of effective leadership. Each perspective holds a concept or question of leadership for analysis and formulation of purpose, strategy, and implementation in personal and professional endeavors. As you proceed with self-reflection and ongoing study, you will develop awareness and understanding of the big picture of your influence in that leadership begins within you. Moreover, the questions center on expanding your pathway and the evolution of you personally and professionally.

This book may be used in the following areas of growth which are not an exhaustive list but only suggestive in nature:

Academic enrichment

Coaching/Mentoring

Faith-based leadership development

Organizational leadership enhancement

Self-study/Independent goal-setting

Strategic planning

Workforce development for leaders/managers

CONTENTS

1
Chapter 1
The Lens of Leadership
Vision

7
Chapter 2
The Preparation for Leadership
Planning and Purpose

14
Chapter 3
The Heart of Leadership
A People-Oriented Perspective

20
Chapter 4
The Resolution of Leadership
Decision Making

25
Chapter 5
The Formal Element of Leadership
Management

31
Chapter 6
The Operation and Advancement of Leadership
Application and Implementation

38
Chapter 7
The Principle of Leadership
Priorities and Values

44
Chapter 8
The Leadership Agreement
Teamwork and Unity

51
Chapter 9
The Accountability of Leadership
Ethics and Integrity

57
Chapter 10
The Statement of Leadership
Communication and Character

63
Chapter 11
The Progression of Leadership
Personal Development

69
Chapter 12
The Sustainability of Leadership
Self-Awareness

CHAPTER 1
The Lens of Leadership

VISION

Prologue I

The higher we climb the clearer the vision. As an individual develops his or her leadership skills it is important to realize that it takes fine tuning and focus. It might be necessary to make a visit to the top of the highest mountain or steepest cliff. Will you not be able to see clearly because of fear of falling or the distraction of successfully making it? Along the path and at each point of transition the true reason for the journey must never be forgotten. Chapter 1 initiates the journey for life which can be likened to a person standing in a stadium or on a field. When you look around the place, length and width seem so large to the natural eye. In many ways some areas may be difficult to see based on your position or focal point. This point highlights the concept of Vision which serves as a foundational start to leadership development. Just as the stadium or field is so grand, our vision must be viewed as broad yet specific to you and me not solely as an ideal but as a reality of what we can and will achieve. In many ways action without vision is the definition of shallowness. Vision is our inner lens offering a global view of time, people, inter-connectedness and achievement. Think about vision beyond yourself and how your vision can assist in expanding others, organizations, systems and life for all. So, let's get started…

1. **Vision requires taking steps centered on our observations and experiences which ultimately make our image a reality. Vision is comprised of vast meaning which is often hindered by our interpretation. Based on your view, what is your image of life? Why? The interpretation should not be limited to your experience with others but furthered through your envisioning of an experience with the unknown.**

2. **One of the most profound influences on the true expression of leadership is an emotion. It does not take much mental scanning to know it is fear. How has your fear or the fear-based thoughts of others shaped or delayed your vision for life becoming a reality? Explain… Through your explanation does it appear that changes are needed on your part? Since our vision evolves over time, change becomes a vital part in its development. Change assists in initiating and expanding our vision regarding self-reflection, maturity, and execution.**

3. **For the longest we have talked about goals as an ingredient for success. However, a goal is not just a statement, but it must be defined to ensure we move in the proper direction. What is your meaning of the word *goal*? Define and List Three: 1) a past goal; 2) a present goal; and 3) a future goal. Are the goals inter-related? Why or why not?**

Vision

4. List five tangible and five intangible changes you have made over the past year? How have the changes influenced your pursuit of success? How have the changes influenced the success of others?

5. What defines your most difficult challenge and avenue for improvement? "Dealing with the Known" or "Facing the Unknown" Explain.

6. What actions do you take daily to expand your vision? Remember your vision is most effective when it remains mobile and its lens remains attached to the heart of sustainability.

7. How often do you assess your progress? How do you assess the progress of others influenced by you directly or indirectly?

8. How do you respond to constructive criticism? Describe how you use the information to enhance your development?

9. Do you give your all each day or do you only give a little and expect much? Describe.

10. What is the meaning of the "big picture" and "small picture" of any task? Explain.

11. Why do some people feel that expansion will decrease their value? What is the purpose of expansion?

12. Accomplishments are initiated through ideas. Are you innovative? Describe how your ideas stimulate change?

13. Vision is a cornerstone for achievement. Are you willing to sit in the seat of frustration and allow time to pass or move ideas from infrastructure to implementation?

Purpose

Purpose is an innate determination, conscious expression and daily resolve.

Perspective

A perspective is a portion of an outcome which emerges as truth through factual evidence.

Capacity

Capacity is a compartmentalized framework with unlimited worth.

Reality

One who avoids reality lives void of authenticity.

Vision

Innovation

Innovation is adherence to a mandate to release inner potential.

Mission

A mission is a concrete task which holds an endless thought, endless actions and endless achievement.

Expansion

Expansion is a conceptual framework of becoming universal in ideas, thoughts, knowledge, understanding, and action.

Evolution

Evolution runs parallel with innovation in the pursuit to expand and transform through insight.

Environment

Success breeds longevity as an environment fosters growth.

Notes

_____
_____
_____

Notes

CHAPTER 2
Preparation for Leadership

PLANNING AND PURPOSE

Prologue II

When taking a trip, it is essential to make proper preparations for your journey. First, you must be clear on where you are going. Once the destination is certain then mapping out the path is important so that time is not wasted on figuring things out as you go. It is very difficult to start a journey with no end in mind. In addition, there must be true revelation in the purpose of your venture. Whether it be for the benefit of others or your own take time to maintain clarity as you prepare. Your forward thrust toward leadership must be sure in order for others to follow. The idea of having others follow you may seem complex. Many leaders feel the need to develop individually before they can focus on the development of others. Honestly our individual development enhances our connection to others. Subsequently, our actions whether directly or indirectly may influence the path of others. As we prepare to lead and live with purpose in mind for the greater good let us continue to focus on planning and purpose as foundational steps which initiate direction for our vision. It is important to understand that seeing an outcome is a presence of mind of your vision but planning and purpose begins the process of forming your vision into reality. Let's continue, shall we, as time is waiting on us.

1. Planning is an educational journey which uncovers voids and inconsistencies and generates continual growth. Name key individuals you would seek to involve in your planning process for personal and professional growth? Will your list of individuals change at each stage of development? Why or Why not?

2. What is the purpose for constructive feedback? Do you acknowledge or seek to avoid the feedback? Why or why not? Explain the impact of your actions.

3. What is the difference between a short-term and long-term goal? Are your goals scripted by your heart and passion or by the perspectives and outlook of others? Explain.

4. Planning is nourished through potential. What is your potential? Is your potential guided by dependability, a sound work ethic and a strategic plan?

5. Plan Assessment: What will you accomplish today? Did your outcome align with your plan?

6. A vision remains in limbo without a strategy or approach. Address the following: If you were

Planning and Purpose

running a race and the finish line is 10 yards away, outline your strategy for crossing the finish line if your current challenge is exhaustion. Is exhaustion positive or negative?

7. Leadership should operate parallel to a desired outcome. How do you maintain momentum in goal achievement?

8. Outline the resources you need to accomplish your present and future goals. Your outline will serve as your personal passport to destiny.

9. Where do you stand with your goals? What has been accomplished? What remains to be seen? Do your goals need modification?

10. Do you have a personal or professional mentor? If not please develop an informal or formal mentoring connection. Mentorship is an integral part of leadership success. Mentorship establishes an atmosphere of accountability and a pathway of quality assurance.

Strategy

Strategy is an instrument of distinction utilized to design implementation, to guide modification and to sustain continuity.

Goals
Goals void of action are mere targeted plans for failure.

Plan
A plan is the central station which infuses energy into a pursuit and solidifies a progressive outcome.

Outcome
An outcome is a stimulator of action, reflection of contemplation and precipitator of achievement.

Strategic Planning
Strategic Planning is a mechanism utilized to construct harmony and evidence completion.

Procedure
A procedure is an ordinance which highlights the path from the unseen to the outcome.

Structure
Structure is an assessment of personal logic used to formalize an objective. Today is a day to evaluate the structure in your personal and professional life.

Information Gathering
The question of importance is resolved through information gathering both at commencement and upon completion.

Planning and Purpose

Pathway

As a leader, other people follow your path. Does your path lead others to belief systems that empower their lives or dismantle their future?

Seven strategic points of progression
These points should maintain relevance as you prioritize your journey

Progression Point One

Sequence: The consequence of indecisiveness derives from a lack of sequence in analysis, approach and action.

Progression Point Two

Patience: Patience is a daily allowance of deposits made within oneself which expands one's open-mindedness to others.

Progression Point Three

Credibility: Credibility is an exposure of oneself to an accountability of the public.

Progression Point Four

Humility: Humility is a time-oriented stabilizer which prohibits a leader from allowing emotion to surpass logic in decision-making.

Progression Point Five

Passion: Passion is comprised of external compassion and internal conviction.

The Baseline of Leadership

Progression Point Six

Confidence: Confidence is an undying seed which blossoms in any climate.

Progression Point Seven

Communication: Communication is a leader's commitment to time in written form, verbal presentation, thought, analysis, interpretation, implementation and application.

Notes

Planning and Purpose

CHAPTER 3

The Heart of Leadership

A PEOPLE-ORIENTED PERSPECTIVE

Prologue III

What is at the heart of leadership? This is not a trick question, but a point made to assist in our discussion of leadership with reality. Leadership targets outcomes but understanding the importance of relationships is a key to getting results. It is necessary for leaders to have a desire to connect with those around them. It is not a matter of feeling forced to build intimate relationships with everyone but to begin to seek a better understanding of oneself. The action is not a single event, but we are better suited as leaders when we engage in a continual process of acknowledging our own reality so that we can become open to the reality of others. It is sometimes easier said than done but it takes a dedicated approach to arrive at a point in one's life when you can consistently incorporate others in your career or life matters. To fully grasp a people-oriented concept one must be very aware of self and know who she or he is before taking on another perspective. Once self-awareness has been realized then and only then can we reach out to genuinely understand others. As we proceed remember a people-oriented perspective is a collaborative vantage point of unity in that the people around us are all stakeholders in the pursuit and achievement of substantive leadership.

1. If the concept of observation is one of the most influential parts of instruction and development, how can anyone be self-taught? Is your claim of being self-taught your limitation and in essence a closed door to expansion?

2. How does your life mission relate to your relationship with personal associates and professional colleagues? Does your life mission promote unity or cause separation? Analyze.

3. A primary element of obtaining results and evidencing production centers on building relationships. How much time do you spend growing relationships with your staff, colleagues, family members and/or children? Are you so focused on results that you minimize relationship construction?

4. How does flexibility to the ideas of others produce harmony in any setting? Is there any limitation to flexibility? Explain.

5. What do you value in other people? Is your first thought of others positive or negative? Explain.

6. What do you value in yourself? Is your first thought about yourself positive or negative? Explain.

7. How does confidence impact leadership?

8. Describe a selfless leader. Do the characteristics mirror your life or approach to life situations? Explain.

9. Do you treat the persons who assist you with respect? The release of respect reveals the interpretation of respect one has for himself or herself.

10. How does your non-verbal presentation influence your connection with others? Is there an interpretation of intimidation, anger, insecurity, deception, peace, or confidence? Discuss.

11. Today is a day to reward the performance of persons who assist in your life achievement. Reward someone with a card of encouragement in your personal life and professional life. Make the action a continued practice.

Listening

Listening is a cognitive journey which travels across the spectrum of time in search of understanding.

A People-Oriented Perspective

Service

Impactful service expresses a tri-fold display of attitude, aptitude and altitude.

Culture

Culture is a precious jewel which possesses an assessed value from the connectivity of the past, present and future.

Assistance

Staff and assistants represent a subconscious perimeter that secures the longevity of an organization. Today is a day to acknowledge the persons who assist you in accomplishing your life endeavors, personal or professional.

Empowerment

Empowerment is a spirit which grants access to the unknown and elevates one beyond the perception of fear.

Subordinate

Staff is not subordinate to a manager or director; however, their supportive role is a valuable appendage to vision attainment.

Charisma

Charisma is a statute which holds accountability to the heart of humanity.

Altruism

Altruism is the imprint of life willed to the next generation not referencing your identity but the anonymous expression of your heart.

Consideration

Consideration is an element of foresight which produces action and outcomes. The leader who employs consideration will always retain an influential resource classified as PEOPLE.

Notes

A People-Oriented Perspective

CHAPTER 4
The Resolution of Leadership

DECISION MAKING

Prologue IV

Why is it so difficult for some individuals to make a final decision and others no problem at all? Well the answer may lie with the person's thought process and how long it takes them to think things through. For some it is only a matter of acknowledging that a decision is needed and not really thinking of the outcome and the ramifications of the decision. On the other hand, others may take the time to consider all possible results of their final decision therefore making certain to think things through so that they will not have to constantly revisit an issue. Both approaches may be beneficial however it is important to realize that regardless of the circumstance decision making is required of us all to get through daily activities from what to wear to who we should form intimate relationships with to establishing goals for the future. The key is not to attempt to avoid making a decision. What happens when we attempt to avoid making a decision in hopes that things will just fall into place? In many ways we give up the control and influence we have in the outcome of that decision. We should not negate that at the center of leadership is accountability to our decisions or better yet choices in life. Take this time to reflect on how you make decisions and remind yourself that each decision you make could affect the next moments in your life.

1. **Describe your decision-making process from initiation to evaluation? Is it outdated? Spend time today analyzing your practices as related to each area of your life? Which personal or professional decisions do you need to rethink?**

2. **What boundaries do you set when making a decision? Boundaries are important to ensure your focus is specific to the issue(s) at hand and you can obtain a resolution.**

3. **Today is a day to reflect on your responsibility for your decisions. What do you do when your decisions lead to unfavorable consequences? Do you reconcile the outcome? Why or why not?**

4. **What is your personal approach to ethical decision-making? Are your decisions made from a traditional/conservative or a modern/liberal view? Describe and provide an example.**

5. **What subconscious voices influence your decisions? Is fear a voice of influence in your life? What is the greatest voice of influence in your decisions?**

6. When making a decision do you attempt to avoid obstacles or strategically navigate through them as if they are doors to hidden success? Your analysis should reveal aspects of your personality. Assess.

7. When do you seek technical assistance of others in decision making? Seeking technical assistance is a pursuit of training which can fine-tune your skills and make desired outcomes a reality.

Decision making requires a telescopic view. Allow yourself to pull back from situations so that you can see the big picture.

Decision

A decision is a future reservation for unlimited potential or undying consequence.

Rational

To be rational is to engage in a sub-conscious assessment of a conscious reality.

Decision Making

Decisions should evidence the direction of the mind, status of the heart, and vision for the future.

Proactive

A proactive nature holds a genetic trait of infinite innovation.

Reactive

A reactive position is a response to the external but a challenge to the internal.

Options

An option is a privilege of a leverage of thought and action between hindsight and foresight.

Suggestion

A merit gained which requires little to no effort stands as a suggestion.

Elucidate

A solid proposal is one which is elucidated with logic, reasoning, passion and purpose.

Notes

_____

_____

Notes

CHAPTER 5

The Formal Element of Leadership

MANAGEMENT

Prologue V

Have you ever taken the time to consider what it takes to manage a dream, a team, project or even an organization? Management is a daily task with all the challenges which come our way? Often, we hope that our individual actions solely would just form an effective and efficient result on their own. Individual actions are to be commended for self-initiation. However, if not managed they become an informal process devoid of substance. Within leadership, management should be conducted as a formal requirement of success which moves people, systems and operations from mediocrity to exceptional. Management is an atmosphere generated by a leader to ensure momentum is maintained for a high level of excellence. Effective management centers on generating a positive return on an investment in a project or endeavor. As we proceed it becomes evident that management involves assessment, action, structure, integration, adaptation, etc.

1. Who is more challenging to manage, yourself or others? Explain...

2. Effective management is a result of leadership that values the contribution of others and maintains an open line of communication to insert diverse ideas into the equation. Do your ideas always take precedence? Why or Why not?

3. What is the difference between a leader and a manager? Is one more people-oriented than the other? Describe...

4. What skills are needed to effectively manage conflict? List and analyze five.

5. Is the concept of change an element of your management process? Why or why not? Change promotes visibility to areas devoid of activity and ensures gaps are filled.

6. What is your view of expansion? Do you see it as creating problems or disseminating ideas for greater achievement?

7. What are the elements of successful performance? Describe: Do you possess what you describe?

8. Leadership is a concept of sacrifice. What sacrifices can you make now to evidence a greater commitment and increased growth in all areas of your life?

Leadership

Leadership is the oversight of ideas, decisions, actions and reflections which serve to expand the capacity of a person's development and to foster achievement within a designated task or endeavor.

Momentum

Problems are designed to produce momentum. As one proceeds with an objective, utilized energy can be replenished through a new challenge. Do you allow challenges to fuel your journey?

Meetings

An effective meeting seals the cracks and refills the agenda to ensure longevity of the mission.

Agenda

An agenda is an inventory of tangible and intangible perspectives which mobilize an objective.

Connectivity to people = Productivity

Is your personality isolative or integrative? Isolation stifles development and innovation; Integration induces development and innovation.

Schedule

A schedule is a diagram of commitment which navigates the direction of one's heart. What does your daily schedule reveal about your commitment?

System

A system is a philosophical view of time which journeys with the intention of starting and arriving at its destination on time.

Evaluation

An evaluation is a measurement of the self-worth which initiates a cause and the perseverance which manages the process of modification.

Commonality

Commonality can be an effective target in conflict resolution. During a disagreement, first seek to address what you have in common. As commonality is acknowledged, an avenue for addressing the aspects of the disagreement will evolve in a logical and meaningful way. Apply the noted perspective but remember the application requires mental and emotional patience.

Risk

A risk is a match between uncertainty and certainty which holds expectation hostage.

Benchmarking

Benchmarking becomes an influential exercise as one takes steps to produce tangible results.

Best Practices

Best practices are concrete elements which navigate activity, produce structure, maintain integrity and value humanity.

Balance

Balance can relate to people, content and actions. A lack of balance can jeopardize or prolong goal achievement as outlined deadlines are overshadowed by distractions.

Flexibility

Flexibility to a leader is like a key to a locksmith; it grants access to new domains, keeps ideas fresh, and sets business in a constant mode of progression.

Laissez-faire

A Laissez-faire approach can produce chaos as it decompensates momentum through an untargeted lens.

Notes

CHAPTER 6

The Operation and Advancement of Leadership

APPLICATION AND IMPLEMENTATION

Prologue VI

On many occasions as a student you may have found yourself completing assignments for the sake of just getting it done without really thinking things through and putting your best efforts into your work. Therefore, it should not come as a surprise to you when your grade is reflective of your work. A good professor should be able to recognize the difference. Ideally your professor has taken the time to go over your course syllabus with you and answered any questions regarding his/her expectations. Attending class and participating in class discussions are necessary to expand your knowledge base and to make certain that you are staying on target with understanding your assignment. Once all doubts are clear the assignment becomes the assessment of your understanding. It is now time to implement all aspects of your knowledge to provide your best work.

Likewise, it is in our daily activities when over the course of time we obtain a grander knowledge base and we are challenged to implement what we have learned at a moment's notice. We should always be attentive to the present situation so that we will put our best foot forward in the future. Our outcome should be rewarding and come as no surprise. As we go about our daily life we should always consider the importance of applying what we have learned so that surprises will be minimized because we have been equipped to withstand whatever comes our way.

1. **Implementation is drafted from a baseline of knowledge. What is your blueprint to ensure implementation maintains longevity?**

2. **What ideas can you restore through new innovation? Remember some ideas only need to be addressed through different means in order to generate success.**

3. **Implementation should be viewed as a point of initiation and simultaneously as a preface to monitoring. What actions are you taking to monitor the progress of your personal and professional projects to ensure effectiveness?**

4. **A best practice for implementation is to engage in experimentation of infusing the vast intelligence of others into the process of developing an emergent strategy. Analyze.**

5. Are you coachable? List 5 perspectives in the past three years you have implemented in your personal or professional life as advised by an influential figure...What results have surfaced from the implementations?

Effectiveness

Effectiveness is a character trait which obtains validity through trials and potency through practical application.

Efficiency

Efficiency is the utilization of the present with a simultaneous reflection of the future.

Delivery

Delivery presents results which evidence the product line of time. What result does time unfold in your life; daily, monthly and yearly?

Details

Details form an index for assessing the distance from commencement to achievement.

Quality

Quality comprises ingredients which are compounded with an extended release period.

Insufficiency

Insufficiency is a confined space which seeks oxygen of diversity, insight and modification.

Knowledge

Knowledge is only a private investigator which seeks evidence through application.

Analytical

An analytical view is a time-oriented jewel which seeks precision.

Implementation

Implementation is a concept which ensures knowledge receives its due admiration.

Outcomes

Outcomes are not the end of an endeavor but rather a challenge for the future.

Application

Do you apply your knowledge or is it at rest within your mind?

Application and Implementation

The next seven points will present a design for leadership.

Design One for Leadership

Theory: Theory is a collaboration of objectivism and subjectivism which forms the perspective for a cause.

Design Two for Leadership

Methodology: Methodology presents the activity of remaining aware regarding the pros and cons in decision-making.

Design Three for Leadership

Qualitative Design: The qualitative design of leadership is a detail of influences on a cause or mission such as history, experience, opposition, human dignity and artistry.

Design Four for Leadership

Quantitative Design: The quantitative design of leadership is an analysis of an objective to seek a concrete path of cause and effect.

Design Five for Leadership

Inquiry: The element of inquiry presents a state of consciousness of variables of momentum which keep ideas in motion.

Design Six for Leadership

Understanding: The concept of understanding is a point of comparison and contrast regarding the growth of a mission, a leader, and followers at various intervals over time.

Design Seven for Leadership

Transformative: The transformative design of leadership reveals an openness to alternative approaches which affords diversification in goal achievement.

No one person can carry the weight of Implementation.

Development Exercise: If you were to build a garden, list the resources and people who you would include in the process and describe why...

Notes

Application and Implementation

CHAPTER 7

The Principle of Leadership

PRIORITIES AND VALUES

Prologue VII

Leadership holds a complexity which makes it hard to define. This may be the reason why some people are hesitant to consider themselves as leaders and maintain that they are best in a position of follow-ship. Where does the reluctance better yet intimidation reside? The question is most definitely valid. After all, during our time on this earth we have the opportunity to reach great heights in life. So what's holding us back? Subconsciously many operate not fearing the title as leader but struggle with the sustainability of their leadership. Therefore, they find themselves making decisions with a focus on what would make other people happy instead of what defines them as a person. Leadership is a matter of priority in which each action is characterized by an acknowledgement of self. The more we embrace what we value the greater impact we can make which ensures our effectiveness and sustainability in each endeavor. Verbalization of value is insufficient if not supported by value-based actions. This chapter centers on our priorities and values which must remain at the forefront of our minds. Priorities and values sustain leadership by establishing a pathway for goal setting, clarity in decision making, effective utilization of time, an appreciation of change and continual impact.

1. The priority of Leadership is to guard against stagnation. Have you become so comfortable with prior accomplishments that your proximity to future achievement is behind schedule?

2. Measure your sense of urgency to accomplish your life goals on a Scale of 1 – 10 with 10 being the highest level: Describe reasoning for your assessed number and detail your plans to maintain or change your assessed number.

3. How do you utilize cross-functional collaboration to develop your strategy to accomplish a goal?

4. How do you approach change? What is your attitude towards change?

5. Progress is influenced by mentality. Ask yourself: Do I perpetuate the past so much that I remain outdated in my ideas, actions, and outcomes?

6. A priority for team success centers on valuing interdependency and accepting accountability for the ups and downs of achievement. Process this perspective daily.

7. Leadership is action-oriented. Detail a personal or professional task in which you effectively transitioned from conceptualization to actualization.

8. Are you timely? Opportunities for success must be seized through effective time management.

9. Does the confusion and unpredictability associated with change generate your fear to change? Tell yourself, today is the day that fear will no longer control me. Now move forward with confidence and faith.

10. Time is a jewel for effective leadership. List your current and future projects and note how long it will take to complete each one. Review the specifics and begin to prioritize time needed for each task involved. Remember un-prioritized time will evidence limited progress.

11. Oftentimes leaders are faced with uncertainty in their personal and professional lives. What about you? During a challenge, what actions do you take? Do you use energy to create tactics to disguise feelings of uncertainty or do you embrace uncertainty with persistence?

12. How do you maintain self-motivation when the outcome is viewed as impossible by others?

13. Do you value others the same as you value yourself? Explain.

14. What do you stand for? Assess your value system and note key points which are important to you. The points you describe will place you on a path of understanding how your character reveals your value to your family, group, or organization.

Value

Value is a mental quantification of appreciation or depreciation through each experience.

Initiative

If there exist any ritual which is deemed good, initiative should be at the forefront and alive as a daily occurrence.

Priority

Priority is a regenerative characteristic of longevity.

Goals

Goals are conscious concepts which highlight character, analyze commitment and assess the mind of continuation.

Complacency

Complacency is a pattern of thought which over time creates an architectural design of self-confinement.

Precedence

The precedence of leadership evokes the terminology of priority, protocol, purpose, perspective and production.

Satisfaction

Satisfaction is an unwritten enemy to the pursuit of success.

Influence

Motivation carries the moment, but influence propels the future.

Reliability

Over time the concept of reliability must become a priority for one identified as a leader. Reliability is a trait of unselfishness as the needs of others are honored. Address the following question: Are you reliable personally and professionally? Describe.

Notes

CHAPTER 8
The Leadership Agreement

TEAMWORK AND UNITY

Prologue VIII

We've heard the saying time and time again, "there is no 'I' in team", but in retrospect the only person that you were able to control within your team setting was yourself. Of course, in order for a team to function you must engage with others to some degree to fulfill the goal. However, understand that if you only focus on what you personally bring to the team then your contributions will not be maximized. We are constantly evaluated on our performance but many of us never really think about how these evaluations affect our team. Little do we realize how the 'I' is embedded within the teams of our everyday lives.

In addition, let's consider according to the Holy Scripture (Genesis 2:23) that although God created man (Adam) in His own image and placed him on the earth, He realized that it was not good for Adam to be alone. This was a season after observing how man functioned alone. Once the evaluation was over, God decided that it was in the best interest to create a teammate, someone who would benefit the team and contribute unique values all her own (Eve). Eve was a byproduct of man in his oneness and God recognizing how much better it could be for man to not be alone. He established the first team and united them physically and spiritually. It is important to note that God in His infinite wisdom knows when and how to bring people together in a specific place in time to create the right mix of gifts and talents to make up a perfect team. As we, His creation, seek Him in uniting us with the right people then it will not be difficult to follow and reach the goals designed for our lives.

1. **Exercise: Draw an image of your ideal team with regard to your personal or professional setting. Explain how the team can thrive if you are not physically present for an extended period of time.**

2. **What is a good definition of teamwork? How do you incorporate the diverse skills and ideas of others into the objective for the team? How do you assign roles to ensure the greatest value is exercised?**

3. **What can you do to improve the morale of your team? Are you vague in your communication? Explain the impact of reflective listening and responsiveness on team building.**

4. **Why do people seek to redefine instructions for an objective to fit their personality? How does the action impact the concept of teamwork?**

5. Teamwork is the embodiment of communication which is open and respectful. Explain a time when you had to discuss the inadequate performance of a team member. What was the outcome and what did you assess that you could have done differently? How has the event shaped your present communication style?

6. Do you sometimes feel isolated as a leader having to address challenges and changes by yourself? Why or why not? Are you still trying to succeed "all alone?" Remember leadership is not displacement but rather a concept of resolve which is generated through relationships with people.

7. Are your team goals reflective of your organizational mission?

8. Define collaboration. Is your definition Self-driven? Does your definition produce results or hinder your progress?

9. Rank the following in order not based on Thoughts but on your actual Deeds: Work, Friends, Family, Personal Development. How is the order impacting your life?

10. Success can be interpreted in many ways. In your personal and professional endeavors ask those involved to define the concept of success. Are the

definitions identical for each person? Analyze and discuss as a means to establish unity.

Diversity

Diversity is the release from self-imprisonment to a limitless dwelling of personal and professional opportunity.

Group Setting

Group settings can foster great accomplishment or stagnate potential. In a group setting, are you an asset or liability? Describe.

Partnership

The partnership of people and collaboration births a partnership of an objective and an outcome.

Integration

Genuine integration is the expiration of selfishness and incorporation of diversity.

Organization

An organization is a structure designed to capture the specificity of utilization of many.

Role

A role is not identifiable by title but through character expression.

Creativity

All individuals are imbued with creativity which serves as a non-fading resource for life fulfillment.

Inspiration

Inspiration is a spirit of cohesion which illuminates the value of a cause or activity.

Collaboration

Collaboration is an attitude which uproots bias and indifference and endears diversification.

Production

In a business equation, production serves as an independent variable which holds relationships as its dependent variable.

Self-evaluation

Self-evaluation is greater than peer-evaluation as it affords unlimited access to the inner core of motivation.

Define Teamwork:

Does your definition entail any form of selfishness?

Vertical Coordination

Vertical coordination involves a systematic approach to activity which comprises rules, policies and procedures.

Lateral Coordination

Lateral coordination involves a systematic approach to activity which comprises establishing meetings, identifying skill specialization and defining roles.

Skill

A skill is an expertise which challenges a beholder for its utilization.

Notes

Notes

CHAPTER 9

The Accountability of Leadership

ETHICS AND INTEGRITY

Prologue IX

Have you ever been in a situation where you were tasked to do a project and were required to complete it in less time than allowed? What was your initial response? I will do the best I can with the time I have been allotted or immediately try to find shortcuts and work-arounds to try and get the job done with time to spare. Consider the auto industry and having demanding deadlines to produce so many cars to keep up with requests and the visible appearance of its fleet on the roads. When the factory workers are pushed to get the job done regardless of the impossible deadlines, we as consumers of these products receive recall notifications for malfunctioning parts and systems. We begin to feel unsafe or disgusted with the fact that money has been spent on something that now has a defect that could have been detected if the proper precautions were taken to inspect or assure that the vehicle was safe before release. We think about the integrity of the company to only consider their bottom lines versus their consumer's safety and well-being. The same holds true on how we consider our own demands and situations. We should not look to just the end result of things, but we should be mindful of every step along the way. There are more positive things to be said about your integrity when you are able to not only be truthful to others about your abilities and actions but truthful to yourself as well. We can be certain that we are measured by our ethical values at the end of the day.

1. Is there a difference between morals and ethics? Explain.

2. The accountability of a leader is connected to her or his actions as well as the actions of all persons involved in an endeavor. How does what a person models impact future outcomes?

3. Is your life value-driven? Values are communicated through actions and historical events which influence future activity.

4. Are you loyal to your words? Remember your loyalty can serve as an attractive force to expand the loyalty of others to a mission.

5. Can you be trusted with confidential information? Why or why not? How does how you handle confidential information define your meaning of integrity?

6. An ethical mind is not guided by opinions but by governance which provides individual and organizational protection and promotes excellence. Analyze.

7. Are your ethical values similar or different from the most important people in your life? Best friend, Colleagues, Mentor, Parent, Partner, Sibling, Spouse or Supervisor. Describe.

8. Ethics is comprised of a persistent cognitive process which seeks to set a standard of fairness and justice so that all can succeed. Analyze.

9. Do people respect you? Do people respect you because of what you do or because of your character? Describe.

Honesty

Honesty is a proclamation of justice and a commitment to consequence.

Do you truly represent your words?

Remember everything spoken is defined through motive and action.

Virtue

Virtue is a moral aptitude which is profound but acknowledged as anonymous.

The Baseline of Leadership

Accountability

Accountability is a personal asset which distances itself from the liability of an excuse.

Respect

Respect is a defining moment of leadership. Respect presents a representation and a cause for others to follow.

Integrity

Integrity references a mantle that seeks a placement of value which compounds with time.

Ethics

Ethics are written principles which are secured through the unwritten and unseen practices of each beholder.

Credibility

Credibility is a conscious standard which holds one upright.

Self-efficacy

Self-efficacy is synonymous with personal accountability to consequences and actions needed for maintenance or modification.

Breach

A lack of commitment within the home setting is a breach to the life code; a lack of commitment within the professional setting evidences a breach to the home code. A combination of the two derives a slow deterioration of purpose and perspective.

Standard

A dividend of immeasurable return derives as one invests her or his all in a standard.

Asset

A profound asset is diversity in Thought, Observation, Acquisition and Leverage.

Liability

A liability is weight which if used as positive resistance can produce great strength.

Reliability

Reliability is a trait of existence which speaks volumes through its presence.

Notes

Notes

CHAPTER 10

The Statement of Leadership

COMMUNICATION AND CHARACTER

Prologue X

How often do we consider others when we are communicating? Is it important to us how they may receive our message or is it more important that we just get our message out? We have been taught to think before we speak. This does not mean that we should just think of what we want to convey but we should also be cognizant of how our message will be received and possible responses as a result of it. We should always be willing to put ourselves in the receiver's shoes and think a minute from their perspective. Many individuals only think of themselves and neglect the full process of communication.

One day we were expecting a telephone call from our daughter who promised to call at a certain time. We being the patient parents and allowing her time to do as she promised did not take it upon ourselves to initiate the call. Not only did the day pass but a week had passed, and we had not heard from her. We politely sent a text message checking to see if there was something wrong with her cellphone. She immediately responded with, "I called you back". We indicated that we never received a call. She being vigilant about proving her commitment sent a screenshot of her call log which showed the date and time of her attempt to call with a message attached saying, "It went straight to voicemail". Likewise, we replied with a call log showing no activity from her on this date also replying to say that we have voicemail but no message. In an effort to defend her actions she missed the opportunity to simply call us but spent more time proving that an attempt was made over a week ago. We could easily place the blame on her millennial mind and her busy schedule but we did not. We only began to think of how often in our own situations have we spent more time trying to prove a point rather than putting ourselves in the other person's shoes and taking corrective actions in the moment.

This type of action is what can aid into building character within us. This not only can create an opportunity to build character but to strengthen our relationship and interaction with others. When we approach situations with the right frame of mind it is beneficial to communicate in a manner that will display our character in the most positive way building a better relationship with others whether it is personal or professional.

1. The most profound statement of a person derives from what others observe. What does your first impression communicate?

2. Where does communication begin; at delivery or receipt?

Communication and Character

3. What character traits have been enhanced in you over the past three years? How have the enhancements impacted individuals in your personal circle? Do persons in your personal circle respect your development enough to ensure your season of change is maximized?

4. What does your communication style reveal about your intentions? Are your intentions self-driven and manipulative or centered on the betterment of all?

5. Today is a day for effective communication. Adopt a philosophy of patience so that you can obtain clarity and present clear in each communication exchange.

6. What is open-ended communication? How is this displayed in your life?

7. What is closed-ended communication? How is this displayed in your life?

8. Is your character expression an asset or liability? Is the quality you highlight as your notable feature the element which dismantles many of your relationships and associations? Analyze.

9. Describe your character? Is your character a paradox between what you speak and what you do?

10. Communication is vital to effective leadership. Take time today to not only receive information from others but also to analyze the feelings or needs associated with the person who provides the information. Do the feelings and needs expand your understanding of the actual information?

11. Uncommon communication is a three-way exchange between the past, present and future. Analyze and adopt this perspective to help expand your life.

Dialogue

A true dialogue subdues uncertainty and releases potential.

Presentation

A presentation is the revelation of self-commitment and dedication to a cause.

Communication

Effective communication is birthed through an intrapersonal intimacy with one's mind, heart and motivation.

Professionalism

Professionalism is not a mask but the aftermath of one's interpretation of knowledge.

Personality

Personality is a duality of thought and action.

Focus

Focus is the priority of time which maintains its position in darkness and in light.

Style

Describe your communication style: How does the concept of being introverted or extroverted influence communication?

Respect

Respect develops a picture of the value seen in oneself as the value acknowledged in others.

Persistence

The resolve to an issue comes through persistence not in a continual query but in continuous actions which evidence the resolve.

Determination

Determination is the pulsation of success which never ends even at death.

Notes

CHAPTER 11
The Progression of Leadership

PERSONAL DEVELOPMENT

Prologue XI

When will you become tired of staying in the same place? At what point will it seem that you have not grown from year to year? If for any reason you feel that it is not important to grow in any aspect of your life, then reconsider. Let your mind reflect on a newborn baby that you have observed. Initially, all he does is eat and sleep. Not much is realized because it takes time to acknowledge that he begins to hold his head up, keep his eyes open longer and tend to make other noises to establish his awareness. If for any reason that baby did not show signs of development, it would be necessary to contact the doctor to see what's wrong. Of course, it is expected that the child will develop incrementally based on research and study of stages of human development. Likewise, should we examine our adult personal development mentally, physically and spiritually? We should continue to expand our knowledge and understanding ultimately to gain wisdom; whether it be from furthering our education, taking up a new hobby or advancing on the job. In addition, we are not to give up on our physical condition once we reach a certain age.

We are reminded of a woman who at the age of seventy-five is still walking five miles a day, six days a week, with no physical complaints and loves to dance on occasions. If she had not set a goal for herself early on in life to maintain physical fitness, then she would be in the same condition as many others who she knows. However, she is the motivator for those who observe her daily routine and admire her perseverance. Lastly, to have a well-balanced life we cannot forget about our spiritual self. As human beings it is important to stay in tune to our feelings and belief system. We must take the time to exercise our faith and look within to monitor our development. It is no coincidence that without proper development in any of these three areas we will not maximize our personal development and potential and therefore miss out on major opportunities for achievement throughout our lives.

1. **Goal achievement never ends for each finish line is a bridge to a new endeavor. Are your current goals leading to new endeavors?**

2. **What are your most recognized skills in your view and from the view of others? What are you doing to expand these skills?**

3. **Effective leadership is influenced by continual mentorship. Do you have a mentor to assist you in your goal analysis and strategy for success? If not, connect with a mentor to assist you in maintaining a mode of success. Track your progress in personal development over the course of your mentoring engagement.**

Personal Development

4. **Analyze your personal associations: Do the persons you connect with foster or stifle your growth? Do they support your vision and life mission beyond words? How do they challenge you to reach beyond your present place in life?**

5. **Since you are a part of the achievement of your goals, take time today to focus on your personal well-being. Adapt a plan for healthy living to better manage daily stress. Focus on things or actions which can nourish your mind, body and spirit.**

6. **Research relevant personal and professional training opportunities you can take to help expand your skills and overall life. Establish a timeline for completion and track your progress.**

Leadership is not a performance of personality but a life of development and endurance.

Enrichment

Enrichment is a subconscious action which is perpetual through observation, study and application.

Pitfalls

A pitfall is a basic interpretation which is best overcome by faith and substantive education.

Agile

An agile person persistently consumes learning and growth opportunities as a means to foster an environment for leadership development in others.

Strengths

Personal strengths are seeds which are cultivated through training, implementation and repetition.

Weaknesses

A weakness is a multi-faceted thirst quenched through the overcoming of one's fears.

Inadequacy

A feeling of inadequacy should not be a punishment but a motivation to achieve the possible through the presumed impossible.

Sacrifice

Sacrifice is the consciousness and appreciation of a fully developed seed more than the seed itself.

Skill

Skill verbalized is success, but skill utilized is destiny.

Personal Development

Knowledge Evaluation (Point 1)

Take two days to evaluate your level of knowledge in various areas of your life. Identify two persons you are connected to who hold greater knowledge in an area in which you desire to expand. What do you seek to learn from them? Be specific. Are you pursuing and acquiring what you need?

Knowledge Evaluation (Point 2)

Identify two persons you are connected to in which you hold a greater knowledge in an area where they desire to expand? What do they seek to learn from you? Be specific. Are the persons implementing what they acquire from you? Is the information or strategy gained from you leading to positive results for them?

Notes

_____
_____
_____
_____
_____
_____
_____
_____
_____

Notes

CHAPTER 12
The Sustainability of Leadership

SELF-AWARENESS

Prologue XII

The two terms, self and awareness separately seem easy to explain; however, the most difficult part of it all comes when you are required to explain it to someone else. This chapter is centered on you as a person and the establishment and continuation of your journey. What makes you a great leader? Is leadership a single event or a progressive phenomenon? As you reflect on the forestated questions you are positioning yourself to better understand leadership from a perspective of wholeness. Leadership is a comprisal of past events, present actions and future endeavors. Leadership is designed to address aspects of oneself which initiate a challenge to mental, emotional and spiritual wholeness. The complexities may be numerous but continual self-awareness will ensure sustainable leadership in all areas of your life. This is the opportunity to unite the independent elements of yourself to establish the developing leader within you.

1. Take an inventory of your thoughts over the course of one day. Are your thoughts aligned with your vision or are they distractions which drive you steadily off course?

2. Are your goals reflective of your life purpose?

3. Take time to assess power from a point of redistribution of seeing the quality in the ability of others. As you connect and begin to respect the ability of others, you gain power and influence in the accomplishment of your endeavors.

4. What is your theory for effective leadership? Is your theory tested or is it only a "blind opinion?"

5. Are you a short-term or long-term thinker? Describe your primary thought at the beginning and end of your day.

6. Are you a liability to your business, profession, or family? What assets do you possess which enhance the vision and objectives?

7. What emotions do you express during a time of change? Is change unsettling to you? Why or why not?

8. Change is a hidden concept of advancement through loss. What things around you, about you, or within you need to change to advance your goals? If you change, what will you lose and what will be gained for you, others, your family, your organization, your career, etc.?

Attitude

A person's attitude is not an outward expression but rather an underlying spirit of self-reflection.

Appreciation

Appreciation is the due assessment of an opportunity versus the ability of a person.

Wisdom

Wisdom is not developed over time but within time.

Humility

Humility is an unspoken word which generates sustained strength and longevity.

Ability

Ability is a craft which gains its dexterity as one becomes receptive to instruction.

Challenges

A challenge is an appeal for one to address any inadequacy within oneself.

Adaptation

Adaptation is a convergence of contemplation, perception and reality. Allow adaptation to become synonymous with change so that you can grow with time.

Practical

Being practical presents an awareness of self, responsiveness to a need, and a commitment to a resolution.

Accomplishments

Accomplishments serve to uncover the internal and external value assessed of one's efforts. Today is a day to celebrate your progress. Take time to reflect and allow your reflection to serve as a power surge to motivate you forward.

Change

Change is a transformation of what was, what is and what can be. The process is a cycle of daily awareness.

Solution

Resisting self-resistance is a solution to success.

Self-Awareness

Legacy

Legacy is not a past reflection but a mandate for actions which shape the progression of thought and values of others.

Intrapersonal Intelligence

Intrapersonal intelligence is a mirror image of the inner layer of the mind and heart and the outer layer of achievement and fulfillment.

Assertive

Being assertive unfolds the value of not wasting time which is the embarkation point of success.

The Circle

Achievement is not a circle comprised of peer associations driven by monetary pursuits for personal security but rather a mission to expand the circumference of life for others to ensure their future security.

Continuity

Will you remain true to your purpose as a leader or will you walk compromised and present an appearance of leadership with no sustainable substance? The prevalence of effective leadership is not centered on actions but outcomes.

Notes

FROM THE AUTHORS

Thank you for investing in your life and expanding your leadership capacity through *The Baseline of Leadership*. The insight sought and gained will initiate and reinforce your commitment to self and the vast phenomenon of leadership. As you continue and proceed through each concept and inquiry your accountability will be redefined from a presupposition of possibility to an oil painting of state-of-the-art success. Indeed your progression through this leadership exploration will evolve the best through patience, consistency and diligence. You are encouraged to allow the leadership perspectives to empower you through challenges and take you through uncharted waters to evidence the true leader within you.

Dr. Anthony and Cynthia Johnson

To write or contact the authors for speaking engagements, forums, seminars, or book signings please note the following:

Dr. Anthony and Cynthia Johnson

Internet Address: www.anthonyjohnsonphd.com

Email Address: AJ@anthonyjohnsonphd.com

Contact: (469) 831-4603

Notes

Notes

Notes

Notes

OTHER WORKS BY
DR. ANTHONY L. JOHNSON

To Be Determined

A Relationship Unveiled From Within

ISBN 978-1-60477-191-6

Relationship Terminology

Daily Reflections for Relationship Development and Life Fulfillment

ISBN 978-1-61215-428-2

Strategic Planning and Membership Assimilation in Faith-Based Organizations

A Guide for Facilitating Organizational Program Development

ISBN 978-1-60477-962-2

Terminologia de Relacion

ISBN 978-1498458078

www.ingramcontent.com/pod-product-compliance
Ingram Content Group UK Ltd.
Pitfield, Milton Keynes, MK11 3LW, UK
UKHW041949230426
12048UKWH00008B/232